MW01709502

ORGANIC GARDENING FOR BEGINNERS:

Everything You Need to Start Your Organic Garden and Grow Your Fruits, Vegetables and Herbs. Find Out how to Work the Soil, Plan Your Garden and Start Growing!

By: ***Aida Campbell***

Table of Contents

Introduction

We hear the term everywhere we go. Supermarkets today dedicated to organic products. Farmer's Markets proudly boast their organically grown foods, and health experts are constantly advising us to go organic. But what does the term organic mean? The answer depends on who you talk to. For many, it is a form of gardening that does not use chemical based pesticides. For others, it means something wholesome and nutritious. However, there is much more involved than that. One dictionary defines organic as "relating to or derived from living matter." To be a true organic gardener, you have to delve into areas that go far beyond the avoidance of chemical pesticides.

Organic Gardening Defined

In its basic definition, organic gardening is different from traditional gardening in that it relies entirely on the natural systems of the earth to grow. Unlike the traditional form of gardening, which is loaded with synthetic pesticides and fertilizers, organic gardening requires you first to understand the natural way the earth's ecosystems support each other and then utilize that nature to grow your food.

Here is a good example to consider. Go to a location where you can look at nature without humankind's interference. Take a walk through a national forest and you will see a bounty of vegetation growing all around you. None of the trees and foliage there has been pruned, fertilized, or watered to keep them healthy. No one walks the forest floor every day, pulling up weeds and raking leaves to keep it nice and pretty. Yet, the natural environment, absent of our "help" seems to thrive. But that isn't what usually happens when we drop a seed in our yard. The weeds seem to jump at the opportunity to choke it out practically. We overwater, the soil becomes dry and compacted, loses its colour. The seedlings we plant seem to struggle daily to stay alive amidst this hostile environment. Most end up withering away to die after only a few days or weeks.

So, what happens when we get involved in the mix? Most humans start to over think the process. We keep thinking of ways to do it better, faster, and more efficiently than nature. Who are we kidding? It's worked this way for millions of years and without our interference. We end up creating more damage than we are fixing.

In most cases, we are the wrong ones. When we remove one element of nature, we throw everything else in the ecosystem off balance and the plants are the ones to suffer. To be a true organic gardener, we need to respect the natural balance that exists between all the elements within that system. When we do this, everything begins to flourish.

Understanding the Basics of Organic Gardening

Many people believe that organic gardening is a new concept. They couldn't be more wrong. The idea that anything organic is new is like saying that eating is new. Our ancestors all were organic farmers. In their time, there were no artificial or synthetic chemicals for them to use so they only had the natural world to work with.

The situation is far different for us. If we plan to become organic gardeners, we will first need to widen our knowledge of how the natural world works. For example, once our garden is set up, we have several concerns. How do you manage pests? You will need to examine your plants daily to see if pests are present. If they are, then you need to analyse the environment to determine if they are a real threat to your plants. Not all insects are – well – pests. Some can be beneficial for your garden. So, it is important to determine just how much damage is being done, if any and whether or not you should do anything about them and if so, what?

If you discover damage that you want to curb, there are several actions you can take.

1. Plan the type of plants that will attract more favorable insects like ladybugs, ground beetles, and wasps to your garden. Planting herbs like dill, mint, and lavender or flowers like marigolds and sunflowers emit naturally forming chemicals called allelochemicals, which

attract these kinds of insects that will prey on the pests that are eroding your garden.

2. Birds are not always a threat to your garden either. Most backyard birds are happy to manage your pest control for you, especially in the spring and early summer months when your plants are just starting to get rooted.
3. Once you know what kind of pests you have, you need to develop a plan to attract the beneficial predators that will take care of those things for you. All without using any chemicals, synthetics, or other products that are not found in nature.

Organic gardeners are also very aware of the soil in their garden. To the layman, it is just dirt to hold the plants in place. In reality, the soil is a living organism that is actively feeding the plants with essential nutrients, water, and oxygen. In organic gardens, using the right type of soil is crucial for success. The earth, or the ground beneath your feet, may have at one time been soil, but is now void of the nutrients essential for growing food. Soil is dirt that has been infused with air, minerals, water, and animal wastes that are needed to grow a healthy crop.

When you are working with soil, you will have fewer problems with compacting and it will retain more of the water to feed the plants. Good soil is the ideal environment for earthworms and other microorganisms that are necessary to grow organic. To find out if you're starting with soil or with dirt, you should have your ground tested for pH balance and nematodes. While each plant type will require a different pH to produce the best results, most plants prefer to grow in soil within the 6.0 – 6.8 range.

For the best organic gardening results, it involves more than just putting seeds in the ground. As you can see from just the few basics listed here, you need to have a plan even before you start planting. It means having the right combination of plants, the right soil balance, located where you can get the ideal sun exposure for the type of plant you want, and the right protection from predators. We're going to discuss each aspect of organic gardening in more detail so that you can have the best chance at making a success with your new organic garden.

Chatpter 1
What is Organic Gardening

Organic Gardening greatly benefits the environment and helps it heal from the damage caused by chemical-based pesticides. This is because organic farmers know that if they take care of the environment it will, in turn, take care of them by providing them with nutrient-dense fruits and vegetables. Not only that, but it also decreases water pollution, topsoil loss, soil poisoning, toxic runoff, and the death of environmentally beneficial bugs and animals.

With organic gardening, it is necessary to recognize that everything is there for a reason. Even the weeds are there for a specific purpose and before you try to remove them, you need to understand what that purpose is. When you understand the delicate balance of organic gardening, you eliminate the need for those synthetic chemicals that are getting into the food. You can use that natural balance to grow cleaner, healthier produce with far less work.

To this end, organic farmers greatly focus on the health of the soil that they plant their seeds in. Rather than using pesticides, fungicides, and herbicides, these organic farmers can use environmentally beneficial and natural methods to keep the soil healthy and also promote the health of the food grown in it.

Due to the care that organic farmers put into their soil, the vitamins and minerals found within the foods grown this way are much higher than those found in non-organic methods. This is due to the organic soil itself containing more minerals and nutrients that humans require. The Soil Association found that organically grown foods on average contain a higher amount of vitamin C, iron, magnesium, calcium, chromium, and other nutrients than non-organic produce. Found that organic produce contains higher levels of all analyzed twenty-one nutrients. The study found that organic potatoes, cabbage, spinach, and lettuce contain an especially elevated number of minerals.

Along with elevated nutrition and decreased risk of disease by going organic, it may also benefit your mental health. Not only will the decrease in pesticide consumption likely reduce depression, but spending time in the garden is known as horticultural therapy. This is because spending time outdoors while working with plants and in the soil is peaceful and meditative. Horticultural therapy has been used in many ways, including to help people with psychological, educational, social, and physical adjustments while improving their mind and body.

This type of therapy was made official in 1973 when the American Horticultural Therapy Association (AHTA) was established. This organization works to train medical personnel and therapists on how to treat mental illness, substance abuse, and physical illnesses with gardening. Yet, even if you are perfectly healthy in mind and body, horticultural therapy may still benefit you! Studies have found that adults have much higher levels of daily stress and anxiety than in past generations. But, by utilizing gardening and horticultural therapy you can decrease your daily stress, improve your mood, and therefore improve your long-term health.

Everyone can improve their mood and mental health by feeling personal rewards from accomplishments. Imagine when you were a child, how satisfied you felt whenever you successfully hit a baseball, got praise for drawing a picture, or got a good grade. Whether a person struggles with their mental health or not, these feelings of accomplishment are an important part of staying happy and satisfied in life.

Gardening can increase a person's sense of accomplishment and reward, as they can directly see the beneficial outcomes gained from their efforts. As a person sees their sees beginning to grow, flowers bloom or bring in the harvest they can feel proud of themselves and enjoy the fruits of their labor. This process can also increase feelings of peace, patience, compassion, and gratefulness, which have been shown to increase a person's overall mood, and decrease stress levels.

If you have children, then gardening may also help to bring your family together. The National Gardening Association claims that gardening can teach children valuable life lessons. If you bring your family into the garden, then it is a wonderful way to teach children the importance of hard work, completing chores, and helping the family. Children can also learn patience as they wait for the seeds to grow into plants, how to handle disappointment when a plant dies at the end of the growing season, and responsibility as they must properly and consistently water and care for the garden.

With a largely damaged economy and many Americans unable to afford basic healthcare, owning their own homes, or new vehicles people look for a way to save money. Thankfully, while organic living may at first appear to be expensive, you would be surprised by how much money it can save you.

Yes, synthetic chemicals and pesticides are less expensive than purchasing organic supplies. However, there are many ways in which you can save money with organic gardening, making it less expensive in the long-run.

While chemical-based gardening supplies focus on feeding the plants, organic gardening focuses on feeding the soil. Not only does this increase the nutritional value of food grown in the soil, but it keeps the soil healthier for years to come. This means that rather than buying supplies to feed your garden time and again, the soil stays healthy with just a little work. Over time, you will find that you are spending much less money on sustaining your garden while maximizing its health and efficiency. This method is known as "feeding the soil, not the plant" as it is more sustainable and will continue to keep an entire garden healthy.

Chatpter 2
How to Work the Soil

The most important thing when practicing organic gardening is to start with your soil. In chemical-based gardening, people rarely pay attention to their soil; they just cover it up in chemical-based fertilizers and pesticides. This leaches the nutrients out of the soil and causes it damage for years down the road. But, organic gardening starts from the ground up. If the soil is healthy and nutrient-dense then you are more likely to have healthy and thriving plants.

Because the soil is the most important factor, you need to spend some time analyzing your soil to optimize it for gardening. This will be more difficult if you have used chemicals in your gardening bed. But, this does not mean that you are unable to switch to organic gardening. This simply means that you will need to put more effort into healing the soil and rejuvenating it with organic options. Optimizing your soil will be easiest if you are starting from scratch in a garden bed that has never been used or by planting in containers.

Check out this list to determine the health of your soil and how you should proceed:

1. **Ensure You Have Enough Soil**

   Many people are surprised to find that the soil in their yards is not ideal for gardening. Many of these yards, especially those built within fifty years, do not have enough topsoil to grow plants well. This is because construction companies will often build the house and then only add a thin layer of topsoil afterward for grass to grow. To make it worse, this small amount of topsoil is often highly compacted. You want to test your gardening area to ensure you have enough of this vital topsoil. To do this, pierce the ground with a shovel and see how easy it is to pull up the soil. You want six to eight inches of easily penetrable soil, known as topsoil. If you do not have these six to eight inches, then you will need to build up your topsoil before gardening.

To create a layer of topsoil simply combines ten percent peat moss, thirty percent topsoil, and sixty percent compost. Some people may confuse compost with manure, but they are different products and not interchangeable. You can combine this topsoil mixture in the ground, in a container garden, or a raised garden bed.

2. **Find Your Soil Type**

   There are multiple types of spoil, including sandy, loam, and clay. To determine which type of soil you have, pick up a small handful of soil that is moist but not wet. Firmly squeeze the soil in the palm of your hand before examining it. If the soil falls apart as soon as you open your palm, then it is sandy. If the soil holds its shape but crumbles upon being poked, then it is loam. Lastly, if the soil holds its shape both when you open your hand and when poked then it is clay.

3. **Learn the Soil's pH and Nutrients**

   It is important to know your soil pH; as if your soil is overly acidic or alkaline then crops will have trouble growing. The pH scale runs between zero and fourteen with a reading below seven being acidic, seven being neutral, and above seven being alkaline. This level is important, as it affects the availability of many nutrients within the soil. Most crops grow well in the range between six and seven and a half.

Along with knowing your soil's pH you need to ensure that the soil is well-balanced with the essential nutrients it requires. Without these nutrients, plants will be unable to flourish and the produce grown will be less nutritious.

To test both the soil's pH and nutrients, you need to take a sample of the soil and send it off to a lab. Many labs will test the soil. To find the right lab for you simply search "soil testing [state you live in]" in your preferred search engine. In some states, you may even get your soil tested at a local university.

4. **Nourish Your Soil**

   After you get the test results of your soil back then you can use the information to improve your soil. To do this, read Healthy and Rich Soil to know best how to adjust the nutrient and pH level of your soil.

5. **Enhance Your Soil**

   After you fully nourish your soil with nutrients and balance its pH to an optimal level, then you want to enhance the soil to improve growth further. You can do this by adding in compost and manure. When adding these to your garden bed you want to mix it well into the top eight to ten inches of soil.

Compost is full of nutrients, but also has a neutral pH level of seven, making it optimal for all gardens. You can either produce your compost or purchase organic compost. Any compost you use should be a rich dark brown.

Manure is also full of many nutrients. However, the type of manure you use has to be taken into account based off of your soil's pH level. This is because depending on the type of animal that produced the manure the pH can vary. Sheep and chicken manure tend to be highly concentrated while cow and horse manure are milder. If you live on a farm and hope to use the manure from your animals you must let it compost for at least ninety days before using, as it contains many seeds from weeds that you don't want sprouting in your garden.

Best Crops for Your Organic Home Garden

Avocados

Avocados are loaded with healthy fats, carotenoids that are high in vitamin A, as well as vitamin E & B 6. Further, avocados have been linked to lower risks for eye degeneration, heart disease and cancer. The avocado tree is in the laurel family.

You can grow an avocado tree in an avocado pit. Still, the fruit it will yield may not necessarily be edible. So if you'd like to eat what you plant, better plant a dwarf avocado tree, which can yield bigger-sized fruits that are either green or black-skinned.

To tend to your tree well, you'll need to put some sand at the bottom of a big pot that drains well before filling it up with your potting mix or soil and planting your tree. Frequently water your tree but make sure the soil never turns soggy because the roots of avocado trees don't grow well when over-hydrated. Prune or trim the shoots often and ensure that you place your tree in a high-ceilinged area because even dwarf avocado trees can reach as high as 10 feet! This means that while you can start your tree indoors, you will most likely need to move it to a permanent home outside at some point.

When the skin of the green-skinned avocado turns slightly yellow, they're ripe for harvesting. For the dark skinned varieties, they can be harvested when their skins become nearly black. You can leave the ripe fruits hanging on the tree for a couple of weeks but if you leave them for longer, they will eventually start to lose their texture and flavor.

Garlic Scapes

Garlic is one of the best super foods around, being a member of the allium family of plants that have a solid reputation of waging wars against cancers. It's also a plant food that's known to help improve blood pressure, lower cholesterol and reduce cardio vascular risks. Garlic also has many homeopathic properties which go hand in hand with the organic and natural lifestyle.

Growing garlic bulbs, especially indoors, may be a bit challenging. Still, it's much easier to grow garlic scapes instead, which can be utilized the same way scallions are. You can begin by buying small-clove garlic bulbs. Choose a 4-inch pot that has holes for draining water at the bottom or you can use a quart-sized container of yogurt that been poked with holes beneath it. Fill your pot or container with potting soil until about ½ inch short of the top lid.

Break the bulbs apart into individual cloves but leave the peel on. Push each clove about an inch deep into your soil with its pointed end facing up. Plant 12 of such cloves close together and water them well. If you're planting in your garden or yard, plant them where there's adequate sunlight. If indoors in a container, place the container in a spot that has adequate sunlight. Regularly water the cloves and make sure the soil stays moist and not soggy. Expect green shoots to come out within one week or so.

When the shoots are about 8 to 10 inches high, which can be achieved within a few weeks, cut off what you need with scissors? As soon as more sprouts come out from the cloves, compost your pot's content and fill the container up with new potting soil for planting new cloves because each clove can only sprout good quality garlic greens once in their lifetimes. So if you'd like a constant supply, you'll need to keep re-planting.

Carrots

Carrots are an excellent source of several vitamins and minerals such as vitamins B6, A, C & K. They also contain healthy amounts of potassium, manganese, folic acid, niacin and thiamine. Further, they also have abundant supplies of carotenoids, which are very helpful for maintaining good eye health.

To grow carrots in your home garden or home farm, buy carrot seeds and if you're planning to grow them indoors, buy a pot or a window box that's about 1 ½ feet wide and deep, with holes for draining water at the bottom and fill up fill it up with a potting mix that's rich in humus up to about an inch from the top. If you're planting them in your yard or garden, dig a hole that's 1 ½ feet deep and wide and do the same as with the container.

If you are planting your carrots outdoors, you may first want to check to see if you have any sandy soil available. If your intended ground is very dense, consider adding sand to your soil in the same way that you would add compost. This makes it easier for the roots of the plant to grow in the ground and you will be happy with the results which will be longer carrots that are straight and not crooked.

Before planting your carrot seeds, water the soil first then plant each of the seeds 1 inch away from each other in rows that are six inches apart. Gently press your carrot seeds into your soil before covering them with a very thin layer of the soil.

Water the seeds and if you're planting them indoors, place your containers in an area with adequate sunlight. If you're planting them outdoors, make sure that the spot is one that receives a good amount of sunlight throughout the day.

You'll know if your carrots are ripe for the picking when they have grown up to 3/4 of an inch at the top, just beneath the green stem. If you still can't see the carrot, gently brush aside some of the soil surrounding the stem for you to size your carrot up properly.

Generally speaking, the saying that "the bigger the better" is true – but not necessarily for carrots. This is because once carrots exceed their optimal size, they start to lose their flavor and sweetness.

To correctly pick your carrot up from the soil, hold them firmly by the roots and wiggle a little bit before pulling up.

Chatpter 3
Sowing and Transplants

Sowing and Planting

More seeds are wasted and more plants are condemned to produce less than their full potential by poor sowing and planting methods than almost any other cultural practice within the gardener's control. Producing the right conditions to encourage rapid germination and growth of seedlings and transplants is the foundation on which high yields of good-quality vegetables are produced. Although this is easier said than done there are certain principles which can be used as a guide by the gardener. If these are appreciated and if the novel methods of sowing described later are followed, then more predictable plant populations with more efficient use of seeds and plants will be obtained, not to mention the increased satisfaction and rewards for your efforts.

Getting the right number of plants

Gardeners intuitively appreciate that sowing too many or too few seeds may lead to a crop failure. Getting the right number of plants to grow per square meter for each different vegetable is probably the single most important gardening operation. From seeds this can be very difficult to achieve. For one thing we need to know how many of the seeds will emerge as seedlings. This cannot be done simply by counting the number of seeds we sow because an unknown proportion of them, often as many as half, fail to produce seedlings.

Getting the plants to grow at the right time

The number of plants established is not the only aspect of seedling establishment which is important in ensuring good reliable yields of vegetables. It is also essential to be able to get crops growing at the 'right 'time, especially when successional sowings of peas or lettuce are made to provide a continuous supply for the kitchen. A delay in emergence may mean a gap in supply. It is well known that seedlings from one sowing do not all emerge at the same time. Does it matter, then, if it takes a long or short time for all the seedlings to emerge? This will depend on the particular vegetable. For example, with lettuce and cabbage which are spaced widely apart the differences in times of emergence of the individual seedlings, which can be up to ten days, helps to give a continuous supply of heads. This is because the earliest emerging seedlings give the earliest maturing plants and the latest to emerge the latest maturing heads, usually a great advantage to the gardener. However, with other crops which are more closely spaced, such as carrots, onions, or parsnips, a long period of emergence of seedlings can be a disadvantage. This is because the earliest seedlings to emerge, which become the largest, will 'crowd out' the later emerging ones, which then may only produce small worthless roots or bulbs.

To sow or plant?

It is usually easier to get a high proportion of the seeds emerging rapidly and all at the same time by raising seedlings under glass in seed trays or soil blocks and then, at a later stage of growth, transplanting them into the garden. This has led to the belief among some gardeners that crops can be established more easily in this way than those sown directly into the garden soil and that the resulting crops will be better. This is not invariably so. Some crops do not readily recover from the damage caused by transplanting. For example, research has shown, even with cauliflowers which are relatively easy to establish, that transplanting may give poorer crops than those raised from seeds sown directly into the garden. Furthermore, some crops such as celery, which are traditionally transplanted, are difficult to establish well either from plants or from directly sowing the seeds.

The reasons why some crops are sown directly while others are best transplanted will be investigated a little later. First, it is useful to understand how to influence the number of seedlings that emerge and establish themselves as plants.

Why are Some Crops Sown and others Transplanted?

Some vegetable crops are by tradition sown, others transplanted, but traditions vary in different parts of the world. For example, in Japan nearly all the vegetables are transplanted even for commercial production. In contrast, in England vegetables are both sown and transplanted.

One of the advantages of transplanting is that it shortens the growing period in the garden so allowing more crops to be grown on the same land than could be achieved by sowing directly into the soil. For example, the same piece of land could support three or four successive crops of transplanted lettuce in a season but only one or two crops from directly sown crops.

Transplanting can also give higher yields, particularly of heat loving vegetables such as outdoor tomatoes. Indeed, with tomatoes it is the only sure way in a cool climate of obtaining good early yields outdoors. Bulb onions from sown crops do not always mature early enough to be dried easily for storage over the winter. So crops are often raised from sets or plants. More importantly, sets and plants give consistently higher yields than from crops sown directly in the soil in early spring.

Transplanting is also used for crops whose seeds are difficult to germinate in the garden. Celery is a good example because the conditions necessary for good germination are more easily obtained in seed boxes than in the garden soil. It is also used for crops whose seeds are expensive such as F, hybrid Brussels sprouts.

Transplanting is more common for those plants which are widely spaced such as cabbage and other brassicas because a small plant raising area will provide plants for a large area of ground, whereas for close-spaced crops, like onions, a very large plant raising area would be needed relative to the space for growing them to maturity. Besides, it would be tedious to plant out the very large numbers of plants required.

The major disadvantage of transplanting is that the plant is damaged, particularly the roots, in moving it from the seed tray or seedbed to the soil. Because the shoot continues to lose water by transpiration and because the damaged root system is unable to absorb sufficient water from the soil to replenish this loss the plant wilts. When this happens the plant is unable to produce its food material and growth is temporarily, but severely, reduced. Rapid recovery from this transplanting shock is essential if yields are not to be reduced and maturity delayed. Some vegetables such as cabbage, cauliflower, Brussels sprouts, and tomatoes recover from transplanting more readily than, say, ridge cucumbers or sweet corn and the yielding potential is less affected. The former vegetables can be readily established from plants pulled from a seedbed (so called 'bare-root' transplants which have little or no soil retained around the roots). Still, the latter vegetables need to be grown in pots or compressed soil or compost 'blocks' and handled carefully in the field. Research has shown that those plants which can prevent excessive loss of water from their tissues and produce new roots readily recover most rapidly.

Transplanting

Seedlings should be ready to be transplanted in to your garden bed or outdoor container after four to six weeks. You can help the seedlings by making this transition as easy and painless as possible. To do this, you can keep the seedlings in a covered outdoor location (such as a porch or open garage) during the daytime before bringing them inside in the evening. After the first day begins slowly moving the seedlings to a more brightly lit area to prevent sunburn. This process should take about a week. Once the seedlings are fully adjusted to being outdoors during the day, known as hardening off, then you can transplant them to your prepared soil.

To give your seedlings, the best chance of success, you will want to transplant them on a moderately cool and overcast day ideally. If it simply won't stay cool outside, perhaps you live in the south, then you will want to wait and transplant the seedlings in the evening after the heat of the day has passed.

Before you begin transplanting the seedlings, give them a light watering one to two hours before you get to work. Once you are ready to transplant your seedlings, you want to gently tap the flat bottom of the containers on the ground; this will help the soil loosen. Then, use a trowel and gently remove the seedling and a little of the soil surrounding it form the container and place it in a prepared hole in the garden. Pat some soil over any remaining holes, leaving the plant level with the ground.

Propagating Cuttings

While you will likely be purchasing partially-grown plants or seeds, not all plants can be grown from seeds. There are many perennial plants which are best grown when propagated from cuttings. This is especially beneficial if you particularly like the mother plant, as the new plant grown from the cutting will be genetically identical. This means that it will share the same qualities, such as color.

Plants that grow well from cuttings include:

- Lilac
- Hydrangea

- Dogwood
- Begonia
- Sage
- Birch
- Verbena
- Elm
- Maple
- Ginkgo
- Fuchsia
- Cotoneaster
- Basil
- Redbud
- Fuchsia
- Broadleaf evergreen trees
- Oak
- Rosemary
- Boxwood

- Clematis
- Cedar
- Lavender
- Honeysuckle
- Oregano
- Citrus
- Wallflower
- Holly
- Dianthus
- Penstemon
- Hyssop
- Thyme
- Willow
- Fig
- Pomegranate
- Kiwi
- Mint

- Fir
- Sycamore
- Locust
- Poplar
- Forsythia
- Jasmine

The season in which you need to take cuttings, the area you need to cut, and the length of cutting all vary based on the type of plant you are using. Therefore, if you are looking to learn how to use cuttings for a specific plant you will need to research how to best care for that plant as it varies from plant to plant and there is no single rule or process.

However, there are a few tips that may help you no matter the plant type. These include:

1. Use clean cutting shears.

2. Do not cut a portion of the plant that has flower buds or flowers, as the nutrients within the plant need to go to the root.

3. When you take your cutting do so in the early morning while it is fully hydrated.

4. Keep cuttings in a cold and moist place until you plant them.

5. Use a rooting medium that provides good drainage and aeration with low fertility. You can combine your own with equal parts of coconut fiber (coir) and perlite.

6. After cutting, dip a piece of the plant into an organic rooting hormone, which will promote the growth of roots.

7. After you have dipped the cuttings in rooting hormone, place them one-third to one-half of an inch into the prepared rooting medium with the tips point upward into the air.

8. Water the cuttings and then place the container in indirect sunlight. You want to avoid full sunlight.

9. Keep the cuttings in humid conditions with a clear plastic dome or a plastic bag placed over the container.

Chatpter 4
Pests and Diseases Care

Pest Control for the Garden

When you are working in the garden, it can be unpleasant to encounter a pest, and most gardeners would prefer their garden to be completely free of insects and rodents. But, the truth is that there are certain types of garden "pests" that can actually be very advantageous to help your garden thrive and grow.

So, you need to identify the pests that you see before choosing to use organic pest-control remedies, in order to make sure that you avoid killing the helpful insects. You can find online guides and bug libraries that will offer guidance and pictures so that you can identify the pests in your garden.

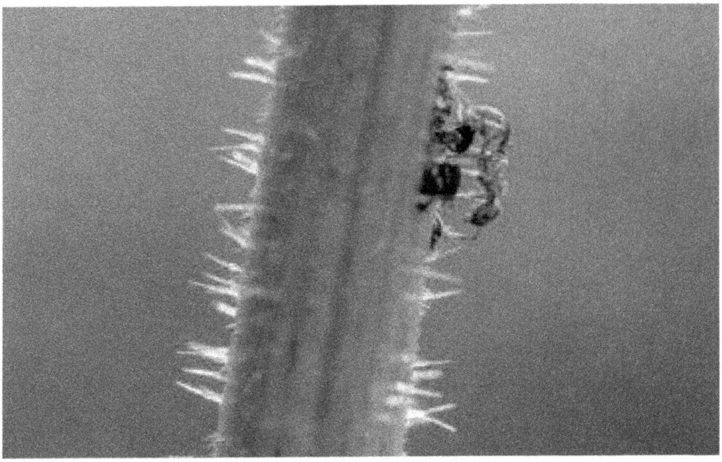

The Main Pests in the Garden

Gardeners often find a variety of pests when they tend to their garden including insects, rodents, fungus, and small animals. Some of the insects can be very beneficial to help the plants with pollination and healthy soil, but other pests will damage the plants. There is nothing more frustrating than putting in hours of hard work in the garden, only to find that you cannot enjoy the harvest because your vegetables have been eaten or ruined by a pest.

The Worst Pests in the Garden

The worst pests that you can find in the garden are the types that cause damage to the plants. For example,

• Mold and fungus problems cause the roots to rot and the leaves to decay, which ruins the vegetables.

• Certain insects begin to eat the plant leaves and vegetables. If the leaves are eaten, then it halts the growth of the plant because there is not enough surface space on the leaves for photosynthesis.

• Small rodents and animals may eat parts of the vegetables before they are harvested, and the vegetables are not fit for human consumption.

• Some bugs can be pests to humans, but they are good in the garden. Bees are necessary for plant pollination, but gardeners do not like working in the garden when bees are around because of the potential to get stung.

The Good Garden Bugs and How to Promote Them

If there are bugs that are annoying to have around but beneficial for the garden, then it is important that you do the research that is needed in order to understand if it is a good idea to kill those bugs. Also, keep in mind that there are certain bugs that may provide an indirect benefit to your garden, because they help to eliminate the bad bugs.

By attracting beneficial bugs to your garden, you can lower the population of the harmful insects. Each location is different depending on your local climate and soil, so it might be beneficial to learn more about your local area and the way insects and pests can affect the growth of your garden.

Following are a few helpful insects that are commonly found in the garden:

• Ladybugs are beautiful and beneficial at the same time. They eat whiteflies, scale, mites, and aphids, so you want to keep them around. You can purchase ladybugs to put in your garden, or you can attract them to the garden. In order to attract ladybugs, plant flowers from the Composite family (daisies).

• Ichneumon Wasps, Chalcids, and Brachonids are insects that eat the caterpillars that feed on plant leaves. To attract these insects, plant members of the Umbelliferae family including Queen Anne's lace, caraway, parsley, celery, and carrots. It is important that these plants be allowed to flower, because the insects are attracted to the flower.

• Praying Mantises are big insects that eat many types of garden pests, and they help to protect your garden. You can buy praying mantis eggs to put in your garden, and the eggs will hatch, grow quickly, and begin eating the bad bugs.

• Lacewings eat aphids and other garden pests, and they can be purchased and released in your garden. You can also attract lacewings with composite flowers, such as asters, black-eyed Susan's, goldnrod, and yarrow.

Best Methods of Prevention for Garden Pests

Instead of waiting for a pest problem to occur, it is a good idea to take preventative steps to attract the right pests and get rid of the problem pests. Here are a few steps that you can follow for preventative measures:

• Develop healthy soil by using compost and other natural, organic soil treatments. Mulching can help to hold in the right amount of moisture. The compost and natural fertilizer create the right environment to attract good insects and repel bad insects, and it also helps the plants to grow strong in order to withstand the potential pests that may be in the garden.

• Plant a variety of vegetables, and rotate them each year. Many times, insects are plant specific, and you can avoid insect infestations by mixing the plantings and also changing the location of crops each year.

• Maintain clean equipment when moving from one garden bed to the next. If you have a plant that is fighting a fungal problem, then you should thoroughly clean the garden tools that were used before you move to the next plant. If you do not clean the tools, then you might be causing cross contamination from one plant to the next.

• Get rid of rotting or weak plants, because they might be infected or attracting certain types of pests. If a plant is rotting or it is having a hard time, then you should pull the plant and dispose of it far away from your garden.

• Clean the garden so it is free of the habitats where pests like to live. If there are weeds and debris in the garden or near the garden, then those items will attract the wrong types of insects and pests.

• Keep the leaves and foliage as dry as possible through the majority of the day. If the plants are always wet, then it attracts pests such as insects and fungal infections. Either use a drip irrigation system, or water the plants at the right time of day so they can dry quickly.

• Apply seaweed spray or mulch, which helps the plants to grow strong. It also repels certain pests, such as slugs. When you apply the seaweed, you are increasing the number of trace elements available in the soil, including magnesium, sulfur, calcium, barium, zinc, and iron.

• Use specific types of plants that repel the insects that are common in your area. You will see some recommendations made for plants that can repel various pests.

• If you know that a certain type of pest is common in your garden, then you can set out preventative traps to stop the problem before it turns into an infestation.

• Sprinkle diatomaceous earth around the garden, especially near the plants and at the edges of the garden. It is not harmful to humans or the plants, but it contains diatom particles that have small, sharp edges. The diatoms are very harmful to the exoskeletons of certain types of insects, causing small lacerations that eventually lead to dehydration and the insects die.

Homemade Organic Pest-Control Sprays

Homemade sprays can be made using water, oil, dishwashing soap, and other ingredients. These natural pest-control sprays can be very effective and beneficial, but you need to make sure that you are careful about the time of day when the spray is applied to the plants. If a plant is sprayed with oil during the day, the oil can cause the plant to burn because of the sunshine.

You will see a few spray recipes of the book, which have ingredients that are beneficial for specific types of pests. Here are a few general homemade spray recipes that can be used for a broad range of pests:

- Garlic Oil Spray is a natural insect repellent. Mince 4 garlic cloves and add the minced garlic to 2 teaspoons of oil (either mineral or vegetable oil). Allow the mixture to sit for 12 - 24 hours, and then strain out the garlic chunks. Then, mix the oil with 1 teaspoon of dish soap and a pint of water. This mixture can be stored in a glass jar. When it is needed, dilute two tablespoons of the garlic mixture in a pint of water. This spray is best used outdoors, because the garlic smell is often too strong to use in the house.

• Soap Spray: Even though it sounds simple, this spray is very effective and beneficial. Add a tablespoon of dishwashing soap to a gallon of water, and pour the mixture into a spray bottle. The mixture can be sprayed directly onto many types of insects, and it will kill them after they come in contact with the mixture. The soap works to dissolve the shell or outer coating of the insect.

• Pepper Spray: Some insects and pests are repelled by hot pepper so that you can use a hot pepper sauce in the spray bottle. Mix a few drops of dish soap, two tablespoons of hot pepper sauce, and a quart of water. Let it sit for 12 - 24 hours, and then apply it directly to the plants that are infested by insects. The capsaicin within the peppers repels the bugs and will need to be reapplied if you see the insects returning.

Chatpter 5
Organic Gardening for 4 Season

Here you will find some specific advice on how to care for your organic garden during each season. Of course, the objective is to garner as much yield as you can throughout the year while also maintaining soil health and sustainability.

Overwintering

There are three things that you can do to provide a healthy winter season for your garden: one, continue to grow appropriate crops; two, plant a cover crop that will both reenergize your soil with nutrients and provide warming ground cover; three, mulch the garden well to prevent degradation of topsoil. Or, of course, you can employ a mix of all three.

Crops for overwintering include garlic, onion, and leeks, you can also overwinter certain root vegetable crops such as potatoes, parsnips, and carrots. If you live in regions where winters don't stay too cold for too long—that is, the ground does not stay in a state of hard freeze for an extended period of time—you can also overwinter several varieties of greens such as collards, kale, and heartier varieties of spinach and arugula. Keep in mind, that if you leave crops in the ground for harvesting in the spring, you will need to protect your garden with mulch and be sure to visibly mark where plants are located in order to avoid accidentally digging them up when you turn your garden over for spring planting. Also, be aware that continuously planting can sometimes exhaust your soil: this can be avoided by continuously feeding your garden rich, organic compost or by giving it a winter break and planting an appropriate cover crop.

Cover crops are plants that you grow to promote soil health, not crops you grow to eat. These include field peas, alfalfa, vetch, and some cereal grains (oats, barley, rye, and buckwheat). The best crops to choose depend on where you are, what your soil needs, and how long you intend to maintain the cover crop. For a short overwintering, field peas and buckwheat are ideal. Not only do cover crops return nutrients to the soil, but they keep weeds out of competition for garden space, attract beneficial insects, and act as organic mulch. If your garden seems to produce less one growing season or if you encounter diseases that are the result of poor soil health, giving your garden a rest with a couple of months of cover crops will rejuvenate. And, when you're ready to turn the garden and plant for spring, your cover crops provide excellent fodder for the compost pile.

If you don't have the time or the inclination to plant during the winter, do your garden the favor of mulching well. Mulch also works to keep weeds under control and keeps your soil warm and relatively moist. It also protects any crops that are dormant throughout the winter but will pop up again in spring. Be aware that different mulches will affect your soil in different ways, and seek out organic mulches, of course, from reputable sources. Many biodegradable types of mulch are readily available and provide the added benefit of being easily tilled back into the soil; these include lawn clippings, raked leaves, or straw. Just be sure that these come from non-chemically treated sources. Wood chip mulches are the most effective at providing winter warmth for your soil; cedar or eucalyptus mulch have the added benefit of being a natural insect repellant. Again, consult your local garden shop, farmers' market, or cooperative extension for specific advice about your region.

Last, be sure to tend to your compost in the winter, as well, adding organic materials to it and making sure it is well covered and continuing to break down.

Preparing for Spring

The first item on your to-do list before the onslaught of the prime growing season is to have your soil tested. Find out if your soil is in balance with the right pH (6.5 is ideal) and whether it lacks certain nutrients (or, occasionally, has too much of some). You can do this at home with a soil testing kit, though the information that home kits give you is limited and does not have the advantage of an expert to provide you with advice on how to correct your soil, if necessary. The best place to get your soil tested is at a cooperative extension service if there is one located in your area. If you don't have an extension service near you, there are resources online. Check out the following USDA resources for links. Barring that, consult with a local farmer from your market or a gardening expert in your area.

Next, you'll want to turn your garden well, making sure not to disturb any overwintered crops. Here's where you might want a tiller if you have a larger garden. Turning soil breaks up any unwanted roots that may be lurking there as well as aerates the soil and prepares it for planting. Add your compost and organic fertilizer at this time, and be sure that this material is tilled into your garden well before planting.

If the soil in your area isn't conducive for gardening—if it is made up largely of clay, for example—you'll want to create your topsoil layer with organically sourced soil. Depending on how large your plot is, you can purchase gardening soil at many large retail outlets—again, look for organic—and gardening shops. This can get expensive if you have a lot of ground to cover, so you can also look to local farmers or cooperative extension services to find out where you might purchase soil in bulk. You should only need to do this your first year of gardening, barring some disaster, as the compost you keep should provide you with plenty of healthy new soil to add each year.

This is the time of year that you will typically want to map out your garden space, organizing crops according to some basic rules of seasonality, succession planting, and companion planting, with an eye on the practical logistics of space, weed control, and ease of harvest. Herb plants that you will snip throughout the spring and summer should be easy to access, for example, a long, squat raised bed plot should promote ease of harvesting with all crops.

Certainly, spring is the time of year during which you will do much—if not most—of your planting. Again, timing is based on your region or agricultural zone but typically, you'll want to direct seed lettuces, greens, radishes, and cruciferous vegetables sometime in early spring, while transplanting seedlings such as tomatoes, herbs, and Chile peppers in mid-spring. For advice on how and when to plant a variety of vegetables well-suited to organic gardening.

Sustaining Through the Summer

Summer offers up its own challenges, depending on your region. For most of us, the summers will get hot and dry—to what extent is out of our humble control. This is also the season during which weeds and pests will be at their most prominent, typically speaking. It is also a wonderful time of year when your garden will be at its most productive, so prepare for regular harvesting and preserving, if necessary.

Most issues that arise during the summer months are issues that are combated or controlled through preparations that have already been put in place: companion planting to provide shade for plants susceptible to heat, using drip irrigation to provide precise watering to the most important plants when it gets dry, and mulching with appropriate materials to control weeds and keep moisture in the soil.

Be prepared to visit your garden every day—once in the morning and once in the evening is ideal—in order to keep up with weeds, pests, and diseases. For some more specific advice on dealing with these. Also, be sure to harvest daily: not only do you avoid losing a fruit or vegetable to overgrowth or pest invasion but you also keep the plants healthy and productive.

Extending Into Fall

The concept of succession planting cannot be emphasized enough, and as detailed, several crops that do well in spring can be replanted for an additional fall crop. The more actively you cultivate your garden, the healthier it will be, and while fall presages the cold nearly dormant time of winter, it can be a lovely time to garden. Pests are fewer, weeds die back, and diseases tend to dissipate.

Fall is the ideal time to plant any crops that you intend to overwinter, such as garlic, onions, leeks, and various root vegetables or hearty greens. While some of these you will not harvest until the following year (garlic, onions, some root vegetables), you can maximize your harvest by cultivating some fall spinach or other greens to eat through Thanksgiving in certain areas, then cutting the plants back before winter mulching; these will be among the first to poke their green heads up again in spring.

Also consider cruciferous vegetables, some lettuces and greens, and autumn squashes as potential fall crops. One important thing to consider when planting a fall garden is when to plant: it is difficult to germinate seeds in the hot dryness of summer, but your plants need enough time to mature before the first hard freeze of winter. While some plants will survive a frost—and some will even benefit from it in terms of flavor—many will not. If your summers are hot and your autumns are short, it is best to cultivate your seedlings inside for a month or two before transplanting to your garden outdoors.

Chatpter 6
Harvesting

Harvesting Your Vegetable Garden

In earlier times, crops were usually grown in the spring season. So before the start of fall was the harvest period. People started harvesting from the first full moon of September. This served two purposes. One, it helped mark the occasion since it was a big yearly event. Secondly, nights were illuminated so people could harvest for longer.

How you harvest your garden, how much you harvest, and what you do with your harvest, depends (of course) on what you grow. Nothing mind-boggling about that, is there? But it is something you need to think about during the planning stages. You need to think about what you want to do with what you grow—even if all you want to do is look at it. But almost every plant has at least one purpose beyond its good looks, so why not get the most out of your garden?

Now-a-days, you don't have to wait until the autumn full moon. When harvesting, the best policy is to harvest as soon the fruit or the vegetable is ready. Just pick it from the garden and straight to the kitchen but how do you know that your vegetable/fruit has reached its harvest time.

At this point, I would like to draw the distinction between two terms that are often used interchangeably but are not quite synonymous-ready and ripe. Ripe is the stage when a fruit (or vegetable) has reached it maximum growth, when it is plump and matured to its maximum capacity. Ready, is when the part is done to your liking? For example, I like my guavas to be a little raw and firm. They are not exactly "ripe" when I pluck them but they are ready for me.

Leafy and stem based vegetables like spinach, lettuce, asparagus and celery are picked when they are "ready" and not ripe. Usually, they are picked sooner because younger leaves and stems are soften and sweeter. Later on as they mature, they get hard and loose the texture. Nobody likes to chew on something for ages. Same is the case with corn which is harvested a little early for sweetness.

On the other hand, fruit based vegetables (like tomatoes) are harvested when they are juicy and ripe. After all, nothing beats a full on juicy, red tomato. This is also the case for most traditional fruits. One thing to check for ripeness is scent. Ripe fruits give off a strong, appealing scent even when they haven't been cut. Have you ever been to a peach garden just before the harvest? It smells heavenly!

Herbs and spices should ideally be harvested as you go. They yield the best flavour when seeds begin to develop but unless you plan on drying and storing them, harvesting side by side is the best way to go. I just grab a handful of mint or rosemary and cut it off. Then use it fresh in the kitchen. The flavor and aroma is unbeatable.

Root based vegetables (potatoes, carrots and beetroots etc.) take a little more nuance. One thing to look for is the root peeking through. If the root starts to show its head through the soil then it is usually a sign that they are ready to be taken out. In the case of roots, it is better to err on the side of lateness. A few more days underground won't hurt but if you take it out too soon, you really can't do anything.

Do not feel stressed to harvest all your produce at once. That's the pleasure of a kitchen garden. You don't have to transport the produce anywhere to sell it in bulk. Just pick a tomato, cut some parsley, take out a carrot and cook them straight away. At home, all your fruits/vegetables also won't ripen at once. So do not feel pressured to "collect and hoard" them. Instead just pick, harvest and use.

The only exception to this can be root vegetables that can easily be stored long term. Some examples are onions, ginger and garlic. You can harvest them all at once and then store in a cool, dry place in your pantry.

For harvesting, usually your own hands are enough. Though in some cases, you might find that having the following tools around can be useful.

- A Sharp Knife
- A Pair of Sharp Scissors

- Long Handled Fruit Picker (if you have fruiting trees)
- Spade (for root vegetables)
- Hori Knife
- Straw Basket

Harvesting is undoubtedly the most fun and fruitful (pun totally intended) part of having your kitchen garden. Enjoy it to the fullest!

Chatpter 7
Essential Tools and Materials

There isn't a lot that you truly need to start and maintain a garden. We, as a whole, have a large portion of the key tools and materials already in our carports and sheds. In any case, if you are starting without any preparation, here are a couple of tips on the things that are generally valuable for gardening on a home scale. The materials talked about right now be key so as to plant, maintain, and gather any type of fundamental garden. Specifically, they are important if you wish to start your own homemade organic vegetable garden.

Top Tools and Materials for your Organic Garden

The essential tools of the exchange are basic and are possessed by for all intents and purposes all garden proprietors in some shape or form, however, ought to be referenced quickly so as to make sure you have every one of them. The top utilized tools in your home garden are tools you might want to hold close to your high-support growing places, as you will probably need to get them a lot for different undertakings. The majority of these tools can be gotten up neighborhood gardening stores and are generally available at a moderately minimal effort. It is prescribed to store them in a place they can't rust, rot or break easily. Likewise, get them far from kids so as to make sure they can't hurt them in any capacity.

Spade

A spade is in an in-ground garden, your go-toto the device. It continues to be used to isolate the soil, dig in organic matter, cultivate, and harvest crops. It's important to choose a spade that's the right size for you, as you'll constantly be using it. An agreeable spade has a powerful handle that stretches to your hip joint at any point, finishing in a D-shaped lock. It merits putting money into a spade with a cutting edge of metal and a sturdy wooden handle; these may be heavier and more expensive, but they cannot beat for longevity. Keep the cutting edge clean and regularly polish it with a record or device, and you'll have a garden tool that will last for ages.

Trowel

Despite the style of garden you have, you will require a trowel. These little spades are utilized for everything from digging planting holes, transplanting seedlings, weeding, filling pots, planting seeds, and in any event, checking out garden beds. They really are a great multi-reason gardening tool. The trowel is unquestionably the work-pony of the container garden and wicking bed.

Hoe

Unless you are like me, you'll occasionally find the weeds in some neglected corner of the garden have staged an antagonistic takeover. A hoe is the nearest partner in battling weeds. If you can regularly get out there and improve the soil between your seedlings shallowly, disturbing the freshly grown weeds, you'll be taking care of your weed problem in a few seasons. Alternatively, you can also use these devices in pots and gardens to create drills and wrinkles for plants. I consider big hoes perfect for planting garden beds but hard to switch between seedlings. I recommend a smaller than normal hoe (for example, a' ho-mi) for easy development between plants if you have the portability to invest in energy stooping.

Secateurs

Secateurs are one equipment on which you cannot afford to hold back. Do some examination and get the best pair you can manage. Whenever kept clean and honed routinely, they are another tool that will keep going for a considerable length of time. It is necessary to have good, sharp secateurs for pruning and harvesting, as unpolished tools don't make a clean cut, harming plants and permitting the disease to enter. I additionally use secateurs to weed a great part of the time, chopping the weeds off at the base and leaving them to rot.

Sickle

Sickles are one of the oldest farming tools, yet just an ongoing discovery of mine. They are a grass shearer like sharp edge on a short handle and are comparable to a stick blade or cleaver. I find them amazingly helpful for harvesting crops weeding, and chop-and-drop mulching. Keep your sickle clean and sharp for an all-inclusive life.

Wheelbarrow

Wheelbarrows, garden wagons and so forth are essential for moving garden materials from place to place. Consider the amount you are happy with lifting, and the terrain of your garden, while picking one. If you have portability issues or back problems, a low garden trolley or four-wheeled wagon is a superior decision than a wheelbarrow.

Organic fertilizers and soil health

There is a great range of possibilities for using organic fertilizers. The best contender for letting your plants and crops thrive incorporate mulch, manure, and compost. However, there are likewise a lot of alternatives you may or probably won't have thought of. Release us over them quickly so you will get a fundamental idea of what could be utilized for preparing your crops if you wish to go organic.

Mulch

There are such a large number of benefits to utilizing mulch in your garden: - It protects the soil from heavy rains - It helps the soil hold water

- It adds organic matter/nutrients to the soil - It forestalls weeds

- It helps to manage soil temperature by giving protection - It empowers and safe houses beneficial microbes - It can improve soil structure and forestall compaction Mulch ought to be around 2 inches (5cm) thick, and a space of at any rate 5 inches (12.5CM) toward each path ought to be left around the stems of plants. It is generally effective to lay mulch first, and afterward clear a space to plant seedlings varying – this forestalls weed growth when a garden bed is vacant and is a lot speedier than laying mulch around the stems of plants.

Practically any organic material which will form a thick layer yet at the same time permit water to penetrate can be utilized as mulch. However, various mulches have various properties, which should be considered when making a choice: Bark chips, sawdust, and destroyed paper. These high-carbon materials make good mulch; however, expect nitrogen to break down. They will really draw the nitrogen that your plants need out of the soil, so you should mix them with additional nitrogen like animal manure, Blood, and Bone or another fertilizer.

Cow manure and compost

These mulches are high in nutrients and won't consume plants or vie for nitrogen. Compost or cow manure is valuable for organic gardens as they are not synthetic but rather 100% regular. Start a compost pile in your garden if you have space, it tends to be extremely valuable if you wish to maintain a larger-sized organic garden easily.

Leaves, Lake Weed, and grass clippings

This kind of green waste is commonly available and generally modest or free. However, leaves and grass clippings specifically tend to smaller and form water-repellent layers, which can hinder plant growth. This can be combatted by laying a slenderer layer of mulch (1 inch or 2.5cm), keeping the garden sodden, and by turning the mulch consistently. These mulches are frequently increasingly powerful mixed into the top 2 inches (5cm) of soil, as this forestalls hydrophobia.

Espresso beans, mushroom compost, and pine needles these mulches all can possibly modify soil pH-levels. They can be powerful, depending on the current pH of your soil. Use them with some restraint to not hurt the plant growth, as they can be very soil adjusting in high dosages. As a helpful symptom, espresso scents will fend off undesirable destroyers of your crops (for example, your nearby neighborhood cats or wild foxes).

Synthetic mulches and weed tangle

There are numerous synthetic mulches and weed mats available. Some are organic and will break down after some time, while others are made of plastic. Plastic mulches and tangles are dangerous in light of the fact that they can forestall water entering the soil and repress microbial action. Organic weed tangles and mulches are typically helpful for ordinary soil science and can be a phenomenal arrangement if you need to abstain from weeding; however, they are generally nearly expensive.

Garden Structures

While most plants will grow joyfully all alone, some need unique structures for support or to climb. If you plan to have an increasingly sizable garden, it is a great idea to have a little assortment of reusable garden structures available for yearly crops. A portion of my top picks incorporates the following three types of garden structures. They are very easy to start off with and will glance astounding in any amateur's vegetable garden.

Garden stakes

A few plants, as intensely loaded eggplants, need additional support as garden stakes. It is a good idea to have an assortment of flimsy bamboo or plastic stakes, in addition to some hardier pickets for heavier crops. The picture underneath shows a case of a bamboo stake development. Extra-tall bamboo stakes are brilliant for climbing beans, which can grow to more than 6 feet (2M).

Pea netting

In contrast to beans, peas grow best on mesh or wire, as the little ringlets they use to climb experience difficulty holding anything greater. Biodegradable netting may be added to the compost toward the finish of the pea season, and hardier wire or plastic nets can be cleaned, moved up, and put away for one more year. My heavy-obligation plastic netting is cut into 5-foot (1.5M) areas, which are stapled to two heavy, wooden stakes. These structures are not difficult to move around the garden and move up well for capacity. In the summer, heavy-obligation pea mesh can be utilized as a structure for supporting cucumber vines, protecting stalky asparagus from wind-harm, or for protecting enticing crops from wildlife.

Tomato cages

Tomato cages are easily the most helpful garden structure I have. Mine is made of fencing wire folded into chambers of 1.5-2 feet (50cm) width, yet a few people use cages made of stakes or prefabricated wire structures available from garden supply stores. These rolls are transportable and strong. In summer, they support my tomatoes and eggplants; protect sapling trees from predators, and support wintertime snow peas and large beans.

Chatpter 8

Planning your Organic Garden

Planning is the best way to achieve the results you want from your organic garden. The first thing you need to do is ask yourself a few questions to work out the needs of your family.

You can start by thinking about the size of your family and the amount of produce you are able to freeze, can, preserve, pickle, turn into jams, jellies, soups, sauces, chutneys etc. and store – as well as how much fresh produce you will need.

What vegetables, fruits, herbs and nuts does my family enjoy the most? There's no point growing cauliflower if no-one likes cauliflower! Make a list of what fruit and vegetables your family likes and uses most in the kitchen.

OK, now write it all down. Yes a list of all the things you'd like to grow for your family and roughly how much of each thing you would use per week.

You also have to decide what space you have available for your food plots. Obviously if you live in an apartment you will have more space limitations than someone living on acreage.

If you are limited for space, consider growing things that you use the most and things that are expensive to buy.

Choosing The Right Location

As with investing in real-estate, a highly productive vegetable garden relies on location, location, location. It is the most important thing to consider. You need to give quite a lot of consideration to the location of your main vegetable plots.

Many poor soil conditions can be corrected over time, but your number one priority should be how much sun the area receives – especially if you are lucky enough to be able to grow winter veggies. Having said that, , Fertile Soil as this is an extremely important step if you want good yields and healthy plants.

You want to aim for an area that gets at least six hours sunlight each day. If you live in a temperate zone like I do, then I prefer to position the garden so that the maximum sunlight is from the morning. I don't mind too much if there's some afternoon shade through summer as our summers are very hot (35°C - 45°C, that's 95°F - 114°F) and dry.

You don't want to have large trees too close. They will create too much shade and compete with your vegetables for available nutrients and water.

The second most important issue is water. Your veggie garden must have access to a reliable water supply. Most of us have mains water available straight from the tap. This is really important as it can get really tiresome carting bucket load after bucket load to keep your garden alive. Besides, you don't want just to keep it alive – you want it to thrive.

If you have some kind of rainwater collection, that's even better. You may need to install a pump though, rather than rely on gravity fed if you are using an irrigation system. Gravity may work, so you will need to test this as it will be different for every garden, depending on how you plan to water.

Grey water (or recycling household water) should be reserved for fruit and nut trees, lawn or ornamentals, unless your water goes through some sort of filtration system. Don't use it on your vegetables, herbs or soft fruits (fruits not grown on trees, such as berries, kiwi fruit, grapes etc.) unless you have had it tested for safety.

You also need to consider how windy your vegetable garden area may be. Some plants really dislike wind, so if you live in a windy area, are you able to erect a wind-break to reduce prevailing winds? I've had tomatoes grown in a wire cage topple over after reaching 2MEtres / 6feet. It's very disheartening.

Consider putting up something that reduces the wind, rather than totally blocking it. When you build a structure that blocks the wind, it creates a lot of turbulence that might have the opposite effect than what you're expecting and needing.

Instead you could use several layers of trees and shrubs. Or for something quicker, a sturdy trellis that could double as support for a food producing vine, such as kiwi fruit or passionfruit if they are suitable for your area.

These options reduce the amount of wind, without the turbulence.

The next thing to consider is your soil. Your soil needs to be (or become) a well-drained, loamy soil with a pH of about 6.5. Now if that means nothing to you, don't despair as we'll be talking a lot about simple ways to improve you soil .

Making soil amendments or improvements is an ongoing thing in an organic garden. Most of this is achieved with compost and the addition of organic matter. Don't worry, even the most difficult soils can be improved over time.

Finally, you might consider having your vegetable garden or main plot/s close to your home (especially the kitchen) – just for convenience. You don't want to have to run too far to grab the herbs to add to your dinner that's bubbling away on the stove.

I've moved house a few times, but I always seem to be lucky enough to have the right conditions for my veggie garden to be close enough to the house and right next to the chicken yard; just how I like it.

Your Garden Design

It really helps to draw your plans out on paper. You can include your house, shed/s, paths, driveways and any other structures, trees or shrubs. Think about any food plots that you'll want to grow perennials in.

Perennials are plants that grow for many years, not just one season. Such as rhubarb, asparagus, artichokes, grapes, perennial beans, many herbs and all of the fruit trees. Perennial plants are wonderful as they don't need much attention once they're established, but give you abundant food for many years.

Having your perennials in their own bed/s makes a lot of sense.

Then you can mark in where your seasonal vegetable plots can go – bearing in mind all the things you need to consider above.

Once you've decided on where things will go, it pays to stand and look at those areas at different times throughout the day (and year if you can wait that long) to make sure there is as much sunlight as you thought for that area.

Graph Your Garden Plot

Use the grid area (click here for PDF) to graph out your garden for appropriate size and spacing. Use whatever scale is appropriate for your property ie. 1 square = 1 foot or 1 meter.

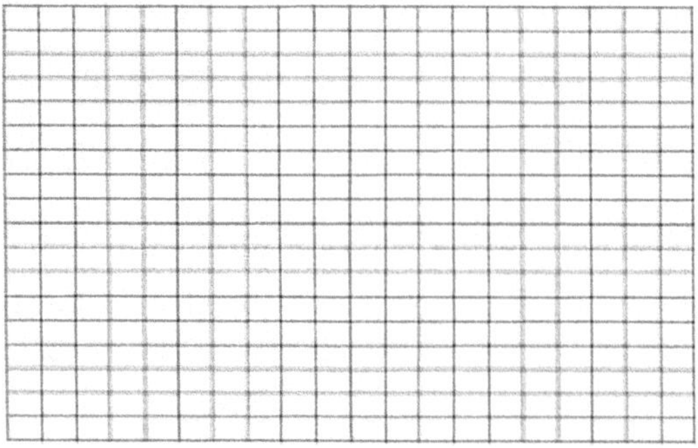

Print the graph out to work with, or draw up your own to the scale you need.

Draw the perimeter (border) of your property first. If you're not sure of the measurement, pace it out and count one pace as 1 metre or yard. It doesn't have to be exact, but close enough to give you a good estimation. Draw the northern border of your property at the top of your plan – so North is up.

Then draw on your house, driveway, paths, sheds and any other existing buildings or landscaping features. You can even include large trees, existing plant borders and lawn areas.

From your map so far you can now tell where areas of shade and sunlight are, plus you will be verifying this by physically standing in various parts of your yard at different times of the day.

Now you can draw in potential plots for your vegetables, herbs, perennials, fruit trees and soft fruits – you plan to grow. You can plan them to go over existing lawn if you want to reduce the amount of lawn you have (a good environmental choice). You can even build a raised bed over concrete if you're prepared to bring in soil.

Once you've decided on where your plots are going and what size they are, you need to print out another graph (or draw your own) to plan what plants you will put in and where.

You need to make the scale of this plan much smaller. Whereas your property plan might be 1cm square = 1 metre or yard, your plot plans might be 10cm squares = 1 metre or yard. Otherwise everything will look so cramped that you won't even be able to read it properly.

This plan will depend on the time of year you are planning for. Most gardeners will spend the majority of their planning for the growing season. For most, this will be spring.

What tends to happen in my vegetable garden is that I start with a planting plan for mid spring (once the risk of frost has passed). Then as I complete harvesting for particular plants (for example corn) I pull out the spent plants, chop the stalks up and throw them on the compost heap, and fill the space with new plantings. This could be a second lot of lettuce, carrots and spring onions. Or it may be more beetroot, leeks and cucumber or zucchini.

Before I know it, it is late summer and I'm starting off seedlings of winter veggies, such as cauliflower, pak choy, more lettuce, broccoli, onions etc, ready to go into the space where tomatoes, capsicum, watermelon or whatever have finished.

Rotating your crops is also a good practice. Otherwise you will deplete the soil of particular nutrients / elements that the same crop planted continually in the same place uses. This also means that the crop will perform worse each year as the nutrients it needs decline and is more susceptible to disease.

You also need to know the right time of year to plant different families. For example: Cucurbits (cucumbers, squash, pumpkins, melons) need to grow in warm temperatures and need a long growing season to mature.

In winter (unless you can artificially provide the right conditions) a cucurbit crop would fail – so leave it till the ground has warmed, the days are lengthening and the risk of late frost has passed (mid spring in most areas).

I like to spend winter evenings planning what, where and how much I'm going to plant in my veggie garden next growing season.

Keeping a gardening journal comes in really handy when I'm planning. It reminds me what worked, what I'd like to do differently and whether or not I planted enough or too much of a particular plant to meet our family's needs.

So let's assume you're planning a spring vegetable plot. Easy to grow plants you might include when you're first starting out (if your family likes to eat them) are:

- Bush Beans
- Capsicum (peppers)
- Corn
- Lettuce (I mostly use the non-hearting varieties)
- Potatoes

- Pumpkin (try butternut or Japanese pumpkin from seeds)
- Radish
- Silverbeet
- Spring Onions
- Tomatoes - try growing a few basil plants close to your tomatoes
- Zucchini

This gives you plenty of variety to start out with. As you become more confident you will try more and more plants and different varieties.

For example, you have worked out that your entire family loves cucumbers. So you decide to plant several continental cucumbers, then say a few weeks later you plant apple cucumbers, then a few weeks after that you might put in some Lebanese cucumbers and perhaps grow an heirloom variety, just for curiosity. My personal favourite is an heirloom cucumber variety called "Armenian" – it's delicious and the cucumbers are really long and crunchy.

Chatpter 9
Maintaining Your Garden

Your organic garden is now planted and in the ground. So the hard work is done, right? Not quite. From now until harvest time, you need to maintain your garden so that your veggies are healthy and happy. When they are, they will reward you with a massive yield that will leave you harvesting a ton of delicious (and healthy) treats to add to your dinner table.

You will learn exactly what that maintenance looks like, so that you can do it with ease. We'll start by covering fertilizers, which will build on the nutrient discussion to provide your plants with the necessary building blocks for a large yield. Next, we will discuss how and when to water your veggies, which happens so often that you'll be an expert by the time of your first harvest. Then we will discuss how you go about weeding your vegetable garden to remove harmful intruders that want to eat up all the nutrients in the soil. Finally, we look at a bunch of micro-maintenance which will take no time at all to do but will keep your plants healthy and happy.

How to Fertilize Your Organic Garden

Fertilizer is an important piece of making sure that your vegetables grow healthy and strong. However, many people seem to think that fertilizer is some kind of magic potion for plants. This results in two misinformed ideas. Some people think that fertilizer fixes all problems; instead of identifying issues such as overwatering or poor temperature, these gardeners increase the strength of their fertilizer and expect their plants to start looking healthy suddenly. The other issue believes that more fertilizer is always a good thing. This is simply not true; in fact it is the opposite that is true. Plants being overfed fertilizer may burn themselves by absorbing too many nutrients but more often too much fertilizer messes with the pH level of the soil and makes it so the plants can't absorb any nutrients. To avoid these problems, you should always stick to the directions printed on the labels of whatever fertilizer you are using and you should educate yourself on fertilizers in general.

Alternatively, you can keep on reading to obtain all the knowledge you need to feed your plants properly.

You could mix your own fertilizer if you wanted to but this isn't recommended for beginners. It is better to purchase fertilizer that has already been formulated to meet your needs. Not only does this ensure that what you are using does what you want it to, but it will also provide you with directions on its use. Unfortunately, even purchasing a fertilizer can be a little confusing. As you're looking at bags or bottles of fertilizer you'll see a bunch of numbers that are different on each bag. This can be intimidating to some people because they instinctively think that it means they are going to have to do math but thankfully the reality is much simpler.

The purpose of these numbers is to quickly and clearly let gardeners know how much nitrogen, phosphorus and potassium are in a bag. These are the three biggest macronutrients which we need to provide our plants. When discussing fertilizers, we often use terms like NPK balanced. This means that the nitrogen (N), phosphorus (P) and potassium (K) are in equal ratio to each other. Most of the time this is what we want from our fertilizer, especially if you are new to gardening. Some growers may use a nitrogen heavy fertilizer (20-10-10) or a nitrogen light one (10-15-15). This level of fine tuning requires a good knowledge of your plants' needs and the way that they will react. Experienced growers are able to make choices because they understand both how to listen to their plants and what each of the macronutrients does.

Nitrogen is used to help the plant grow. While the roots get some benefit from this, it is the leaves and foliage that gain the biggest boost. You can identify a lack of nitrogen in a plant by the way its leaves turn an autumn yellow while the rest of the plant lightens and takes on a sickly shade of green. But while a plant needs nitrogen, it will die if it gets too much. Phosphorus, on the other hand, is much more involved in growing roots and fruit. Too little of it and your plants will produce a poor yield or even fail to grow to regular size. Finally, potassium is used for more esoteric purposes such as the various chemical processes which are happening inside of the plant at any given second. Yellow leaves and a failure to grow result from too little potassium, which is a major pain as it can be easy to misdiagnose a potassium shortage as a shortage of either nitrogen or phosphorus.

There are two ways to apply fertilizer. Most indoor or raised bed gardeners use a liquid fertilizer. This is made by purchasing either a liquid mixture that is diluted with water or a mixture of raw materials which is then dissolved in water. This is sprayed or poured onto the soil around the plants. However, many outdoor gardeners prefer to go with a solid fertilizer which is mixed into the soil itself. One way of doing this is to mix fertilizer in with the soil as you are making rows but before anything has been planted. When done in this way, the fertilizer is mixed to be spread out throughout the soil but under the top few feet so that the plants' roots can find it as they grow. Another way is to pour a line of fertilizer along the side of the row.

The best way to determine how often and how much fertilizer to give your plants is to follow the instructions on the package. Many gardeners will start their plants off with a smaller dosage to see how they respond to it before mixing it stronger and stronger until it is at the level recommended on the package.

It should be noted that solid fertilizers don't need to be used on a weekly basis. This is the scheduling for a liquid fertilizer, which I recommend for beginners because it is harder to make mistakes with it. You could over feed your plants, but as long as you are following the instructions it is unlikely that you will. However, a solid fertilizer can prove harmful to your plants, as direct contact with the roots while they are still young could actually just straight out kill your plants. If you use a liquid fertilizer and you are careful to follow the instructions, this won't be a problem for you. You can always branch out and start experimenting with other kinds of fertilizers after you get a feeling for how fertilizer changes the pH level of the soil and affects your vegetables. Just remember not to apply fertilizer directly to the plants but rather to the soil around them.

Watering Your Vegetable Garden

Watering the plants is another one of the images that pop into people's minds when they think about gardening. Everyone knows that plants need water, though it seems that not everybody realizes just how much. Hydrogen is one of the macronutrients which plants need to live but too much hydrogen causes root rot and leaves your plants sick.

Too little water also leaves them sick, though it is typically better to err on the side of too little than too much. Your plants use visual signs in order to communicate their needs to you. One of the clear ways that plants tell us they need water is to start wilting. However, before you go watering them, you need to make sure that the reason they are wilting is the lack of water. If you notice your plants are wilting around noon, avoid watering them right away. This is the time of day when the sun is at its hottest and it may be the heat that is causing the wilt. Wait a couple hours and see if your plants bounce back as the temperature cools off. If they don't, then they probably do need watering. If they do bounce back, wilting was actually a part of the way that the plants withstand their environment. Midday wilting is the plant equivalent to people sweating a lot in the heat.

The reason you want to make sure your plants are wilting due to lack of water and not just midday heat is so that you aren't overwatering them. Your plants will give you clear signs that they are underwatered but the signs of overwatering can easily be missed if you aren't looking for them. Too much water may cause your plants to wilt as well, so remember to check the soil before watering (we'll see how this is done in a moment). Another sign is that the leaves of the plant will start to turn a brownish color and then wilt. If your plants are showing this combination of brown leaves and wilting then you can be reasonably sure that overwatering is at fault. Another sign is to look for edema, which is a condition that happens when a plant has drank too much water and its cells begin to rupture and burst. Edema shows up kind of like a blister on the leaves of the plant, though it may also look like bruises. Yellow leaves that start to fall off of the plant might be a sign of overwatering but it can be easy to misdiagnose them as a sign that there isn't enough nitrogen being absorbed. Finally, root rot in the big one that you need to be worried about, but this starts in the roots and these are hidden from view. Root rot spreads throughout the rest of the plant, but usually by the time it enters into the foliage it is too late.

Of course, underwatering your plant can also easily kill it but most gardeners don't have a problem with underwatering. It is overwatering that does the most harm, especially to beginners who haven't done their research. It has been said a thousand times already in this book: if you want to be a gardening pro, then you need to get used to doing research. It takes next to no time and it can stop you from making deadly choices.

How often you should be watering your vegetables is going to be determined by four factors: the soil you are using, the temperature of your local climate, whether your veggies are getting full sun or shade, and the species of veggie you are growing. Oftentimes you can collapse those last two factors together because a vegetable needs a specific amount of sun or shade but there is enough variation there to make it worth the extra note. We'll discuss how these factors interact before moving on to how to tell it is time to water and how to water your plants when they are ready properly.

Out of the four factors above, the species of vegetable you are growing is going to be the most important. However, it is also the one that is the hardest to write about because of the endless variation therein. We can look to the vegetables to get an idea of how this changes. Carrots require weekly watering. Broccoli likes to be watered once or twice a week. Peppers like two waterings a week, same as lettuce. Tomatoes like a lot of water, twice a week. These are all pretty close to each other but you can see how carrots would be overwatered if you treated them like tomatoes. The species you are going with is your starting point; the other three factors will then alter the schedule.

Chatpter 10 Organic Gardening Tips and Tricks

There are many tips and tricks that can help the organic gardener improve their garden, increase their harvest, and more. We will go over some of the more helpful tips that you may find beneficial in your daily life.

1. Recycle when Sowing Seeds

You can certainly go to the local garden center and buy seed starters to help you sprout your small seeds. But, these are pricier than you have to pay, especially considering that many people have objects around their house that they could recycle. Why pay for more plastic to end up in landfills when you could instead repurpose something you already own but don't need? There are everyday items such as egg cartons, eggshells, citrus peels, empty K-cup containers, bathroom cups, and more.

2. Become Familiar with Organic Fertilizers

There are certainly organic fertilizers on the market. But, rather than using pre-made organic fertilizers, you can make your own. By mixing up your own fertilizer, you can save money and customize it to your garden's needs. There are many options such as compost, tea, Epsom salt, seaweed, and fish emulsions.

3. Recycle Eggshells

There are many nutrients inside an egg. While you are unable to compost eggs themselves for your garden, there are many benefits to adding eggshells. After you use the egg from within the shell, clean and dry the shells before grinding them up. You can then add them to your compost pile or directly to your garden for an increase in calcium.

4. Using Epsom Salt

If you are someone who is interested in living naturally and organically, you probably already love Epsom salt. But, if you are unfamiliar with this amazing product you may want to try using it more.

This salt, while great for human use, is also helpful in the garden. By adding this salt to your soil, you can feed your plants nutrients and decrease the shock produced from transplantation. Better yet, this salt can keep pests such as slugs away!

5. Use Essential Oils

Essential oils don't only have to be used on humans! While you shouldn't typically use these oils on animals, there are many beneficial ways you can use them in your garden bed. After all, these oils are derived from plant life and can, in turn, feed more plant life to grow stronger in the future. Why not try using rosemary or peppermint oil to rid your garden of pests? Tea tree oil is powerful against fighting off fungal diseases. Pine will ward off slugs. Peppermint will keep mice and other animals away. And, neroli and lavender will attract bees!

6. Fight Insects with Insects

Pest control is a big concern for many people when gardening, for a good reason. These small bugs and insects can quickly kill a crop. But, it doesn't have to be this way. There are many safe and effective ways in which you can fight off damaging insects such as slugs, aphids, and caterpillars. While there are many options, one of the best and easiest ways to fight off these damaging insects is to introduce their natural predators, helpful insects. You can learn what to plant in order to fight off specific insects you are having problems with directly. For instance, if you plant basil next to tomatoes it can help ward off tomato hornworms. Learn more about using cohort plants that will draw to your garden helpful insects while repelling harmful insects.

7. Rid Your Garden of Aphids

While there are many insects that can destroy crops, one of the worst out there are aphids. These tiny little insects come in the thousands to eat and destroy your harvest and flowers. While you may try to use organic pesticides, these tiny insects have a hard waxy coating on their bodies which protects them from most of these pesticides. Worse yet, they reproduce shockingly fast, making them even harder to rid yourself of. Thankfully, you don't have to let aphids kill your garden.

First, you can add some neem essential oil to water and spray it onto any plants that aphids are attacking. However, avoid spraying plants not affected by aphids, as the neem oil may also cause beneficial insects to keep away.

The larvae of green lacewings eat aphids and are one of the best ways to rid your garden of these pests. To draw lacewings to your garden try planting dill, caraway, cilantro, and fennel. Ladybugs are another helpful insect to keep away the aphids. To draw this cute little bug to your garden plant dill, butterfly weed, cilantro, Queen Anne's lace, and fennel. Lastly, you will want to attract hoverflies to eat the aphids. In order to attract these insects plant dill, caraway, cilantro, fennel, English lavender, lemon balm, spearmint, parsley, and wild bergamot.

8. Keep the Bites at Bay

Gardening is peaceful and relaxing... that is until you begin to get mosquito bites and bugs swarming around you. To save yourself during this season try using natural bug repellents and bug sprays rather than the strongly scented chemical sprays sold at stores.

In order to create a natural bug repellent, combine two ounces of grapeseed or coconut oil in a container with five drops of peppermint, three drops of lavender, three drops of tea tree, two drops of citronella, and lastly four drops of vetiver essential oil. After the mixture is combined you can rub the oil onto your limbs and neck to keep the bugs at bay while you work on your gardening.

9. Feed the Microbes

There are billions of microbes within the soil, which is just as important as the nutrients within the soil. You need to feed these microbes, which include algae, fungi, bacteria, protozoa, and actinomycetes. In order to feed these microbes, combine a gallon of water with a quarter cup of molasses and four cups of compost. Pour this mixture over the garden bed before fully watering the soil. This will allow the mixture to be absorbed deeply by the soil fully, and the molasses will feed the beneficial microbes.

10. Aerate Your Compost

We've talked a lot about how aerating your compost is important. But, a simple trick to improve the air within a new compost heap is to start your pile on top of a bed of sticks and branches. In the center of the pile, place a PVC pipe with holes drilled in its sides, sticking it partially in the ground so it sticks straight up in the air. Place your compost ingredients around the pipe and on top of the sticks and branches, which will increase air flow and therefore helps reduce the time it takes for the ingredients to become fully composted.

11. Invite Toads Over

Toads are wonderful at controlling pests in your garden. They eat plenty of bad bugs and keep the harmful slugs and snails away. Try to attract toads to your garden by adding a little "pond" and a house for them. This pond can be a simple dish that you fill with water and place in a hole in the ground. While toads may not live in the water, they still need a wet environment. This pan of water will give them just what they need. Toads also need cover from the sun and predators, therefore making them a simple house. You can easily build this house by placing an upside-down broken pot on the ground. The pot will need to have a hole in it that is big enough for toads to use as an entrance and exit.

12. Grow Marigolds

Both American and French marigolds are wonderful at killing harmful pests known as nematodes. These are pests that are microscopic, but live in the soil and causes damage to potatoes, tomatoes, and many other crops. Thankfully, the roots of marigolds and their decaying leaves and flowers release chemicals within the soil that kill nematodes. If you plant these flowers around plants that are susceptible to nematodes you can protect them.

13. Rotate Crops

Plants that are in the same family and closely related are often affected by the same diseases. If you continue to grow plants from the same family in the same location year after year, they can develop diseases and reduce nutrients within the soil. This is especially true for nightshades such as tomatoes, peppers, potatoes, eggplants and squash family which contains summer and winter squash, cucumber, and watermelon. Therefore, to increase nutrients and prevent disease it is best to rotate crops from year to year. For instance, don't plant nightshades in the same location each year, move them to another portion of your garden and plant another type of vegetable where they had grown.

14. Prioritize Cleanliness

When leaves and flowers fall off of the plants in your garden, they can quickly become diseases and infect your other plants with fungi or bacteria. Therefore, walk through your garden daily and pick up any fallen foliage you see to prevent this disease.

Chatpter 11
Starting Your Seeds

Harvesting seeds is only half the battle. When spring comes around, you have to be able to start those seeds so they can be planted.

You're going to need some supplies. Here's list of basic supplies you'll need to get your seeds going:

• Containers. You're going to need something to start your seeds in. You can buy flats that will hold multiple seeds. In a pinch, you can use egg cartons or even a bucket in which you start multiple seeds.

- Organic potting mix. You're going to need potting mix to start your seeds in. You can buy potting mix or make it by mixing equal parts of compost, vermiculite and sphagnum peat moss. In a pinch, you can use garden soil, but potting soil is preferable.
- Seeds. You can't start seeds if you don't have any.
- Plastic sheets. Plastic can be used to increase warmth.
- Water. Seeds won't grow in soil that's too dry.
- Light. Fluorescent lights and sunlight work best.

Here are the steps you need to follow to get your seeds started:

1. Break up your potting mix.

Potting soil tends to clump up. Breaking it up will ensure water is spread evenly throughout the soil. It also allows the root of your plants to push their way through the soil more easily.

2. Dampen the soil.

You want your soil to be damp, but not soaking wet. There shouldn't be any dry patches. Stir your soil up to ensure moisture is evenly distributed.

3. Add the soil to your containers.

This step is self-explanatory. Add your soil to your potting containers. Fill them up and shake them a little to allow the soil to settle. You want it to be careful and loose instead of tightly packed.

4. Wash and plant your seeds according to the best practices for your seed type.

This is easy if you're planting seeds from a package. All you have to do is follow the instructions on the package

If you're unable to find information on your particular seed type, the following instructions should help you get your seeds started:

spot, pick the most muscular looking one and cull the rest.

10. Once it's time to plant your seedlings outdoors, move them to your garden.

Conclusion

Thank you for making it to the end. It is healthy to grow your own organic garden and there are a plethora of benefits, as mentioned above, for doing so. Gardening is beneficial for the mind, body and soul. There are also many excellent reasons to employ organic gardening practices when it comes to growing food and even flowers.

Organic gardening creates a safe environment for plants, animals and gardeners. When you practice organic gardening you tread lightly on the earth and you care about not only your own health but the health of your family members, pets, wildlife and the planet.

Organic gardening practices are not new; in fact they are quite possibly the way your grandparents or great grandparents gardened. Prior to the onslaught of chemicals, hybrid seeds and "big business" as we know it today, organic gardening was commonplace and well understood.

Today, many gardeners are going back to these time-tested methods of gardening including using organic fertilizers, organic pesticides and a variety of chemical-free ways to keep plants healthy and harvests bountiful.

The philosophy of organic gardening includes an understanding of a plant's natural defense mechanisms and ways that the gardener can best support these innate characteristics. Very much like holistic health, organic gardening considers all parts of the garden and utilizes natural methods to manage and tend the garden plants.

The secrets in this book are organic because we believe this is the best and safest way to garden. Organic gardening is the best possible way for you to connect with the earth and makes the entire gardening experience as rewarding as possible.

Growing our own food is unquestionably among the most helpful pastimes in our own lives. We develop food in our garden, crop it and consume it minutes ter. Raised together with our own hands, cooked and prepared thickly -- what more can we wish for? Most of us are aware of the health benefits of vegetables. You could even clap your shoulders in cutting air miles. There's surely no petroleum wasted in importing vegetables which come from throughout the world.

When we develop our own food, we understand exactly what's gone into developing it. Lots of men and women worry about pesticide residues in food. Even if science demonstrates these pesticide residues from foods are totally harmless since they're under a particular threshold, a lot of individuals simply prefer to consume food which has rose naturally with no artificial inputs and hopefully rose by them. Personally, I'm a dedicated organic gardener and I never utilized synthetic fertilizers or synthetic pesticides and that I believe there's not any demand for this. Nature itself takes care of this, as an older gardening buddy said: 'Plants only need to grow'.

Gardening makes us modest. The food that we grow is raised by Mother Earth and can be given to us as a present. Even after 25 decades of growing veggies I still encounter these small wonders of sowing a seed or planting a seed curry and then seeing the revelation.

Until not that long ago, each Family needed to develop their own meals. If the plants failed, they needed to perform with less and when the plants did well there was a massive sense of satisfaction. There was a powerful sense of purpose of placing food on the table to your family. We no longer possess this feeling of purpose within our Contemporary lives.

I hope you have learned something!

CPSIA information can be obtained
at www.ICGtesting.com
Printed in the USA
BVHW041826090221
599737BV00023B/309

9 781801 096867